The art of Playing at Skittles: or, the Laws of Nine-pins Displayed. Shewing Both the old and new Methods of Forming General Goes and Tips, ... Also an Address to Publicans, ... By A. Jones, Esq

The art of playing at skittles: or, the laws of nine-pins displayed. Shewing both the old and new methods of forming general goes and tips, ... Also an address to publicans, ... By A. Jones, Esq.
Jones, A.
ESTCID: T082586
Reproduction from British Library
With two final advertisement leaves.
London : printed for the author, and sold by J. Wilkie, 1773.
56,[4]p. ; 12°

ECCO

Eighteenth Century Collections Online Print Editions

Gale ECCO Print Editions

Relive history with *Eighteenth Century Collections Online*, now available in print for the independent historian and collector. This series includes the most significant English-language and foreign-language works printed in Great Britain during the eighteenth century, and is organized in seven different subject areas including literature and language; medicine, science, and technology; and religion and philosophy. The collection also includes thousands of important works from the Americas.

The eighteenth century has been called "The Age of Enlightenment." It was a period of rapid advance in print culture and publishing, in world exploration, and in the rapid growth of science and technology – all of which had a profound impact on the political and cultural landscape. At the end of the century the American Revolution, French Revolution and Industrial Revolution, perhaps three of the most significant events in modern history, set in motion developments that eventually dominated world political, economic, and social life.

In a groundbreaking effort, Gale initiated a revolution of its own: digitization of epic proportions to preserve these invaluable works in the largest online archive of its kind. Contributions from major world libraries constitute over 175,000 original printed works. Scanned images of the actual pages, rather than transcriptions, recreate the works ***as they first appeared.***

Now for the first time, these high-quality digital scans of original works are available via print-on-demand, making them readily accessible to libraries, students, independent scholars, and readers of all ages.

For our initial release we have created seven robust collections to form one the world's most comprehensive catalogs of 18th century works.

Initial Gale ECCO Print Editions collections include:

History and Geography
Rich in titles on English life and social history, this collection spans the world as it was known to eighteenth-century historians and explorers. Titles include a wealth of travel accounts and diaries, histories of nations from throughout the world, and maps and charts of a world that was still being discovered. Students of the War of American Independence will find fascinating accounts from the British side of conflict.

Social Science

Delve into what it was like to live during the eighteenth century by reading the first-hand accounts of everyday people, including city dwellers and farmers, businessmen and bankers, artisans and merchants, artists and their patrons, politicians and their constituents. Original texts make the American, French, and Industrial revolutions vividly contemporary.

Medicine, Science and Technology

Medical theory and practice of the 1700s developed rapidly, as is evidenced by the extensive collection, which includes descriptions of diseases, their conditions, and treatments. Books on science and technology, agriculture, military technology, natural philosophy, even cookbooks, are all contained here.

Literature and Language

Western literary study flows out of eighteenth-century works by Alexander Pope, Daniel Defoe, Henry Fielding, Frances Burney, Denis Diderot, Johann Gottfried Herder, Johann Wolfgang von Goethe, and others. Experience the birth of the modern novel, or compare the development of language using dictionaries and grammar discourses.

Religion and Philosophy

The Age of Enlightenment profoundly enriched religious and philosophical understanding and continues to influence present-day thinking. Works collected here include masterpieces by David Hume, Immanuel Kant, and Jean-Jacques Rousseau, as well as religious sermons and moral debates on the issues of the day, such as the slave trade. The Age of Reason saw conflict between Protestantism and Catholicism transformed into one between faith and logic -- a debate that continues in the twenty-first century.

Law and Reference

This collection reveals the history of English common law and Empire law in a vastly changing world of British expansion. Dominating the legal field is the *Commentaries of the Law of England* by Sir William Blackstone, which first appeared in 1765. Reference works such as almanacs and catalogues continue to educate us by revealing the day-to-day workings of society.

Fine Arts

The eighteenth-century fascination with Greek and Roman antiquity followed the systematic excavation of the ruins at Pompeii and Herculaneum in southern Italy; and after 1750 a neoclassical style dominated all artistic fields. The titles here trace developments in mostly English-language works on painting, sculpture, architecture, music, theater, and other disciplines. Instructional works on musical instruments, catalogs of art objects, comic operas, and more are also included.

THE

A R T

OF

PLAYING AT SKITTLES:

OR, THE

Laws of Nine-Pins diſplayed.

SHEWING

Both the OLD and NEW Methods of forming General *Goes* and *Tips*, with the Names, Counts, and Exceptions to each.

TO WHICH ARE ADDED,

The CHINESE and PERSIAN Manner of Playing; illuſtrated with Diagrams, Plans, &c. of the ſeveral Frames and Grounds, both in the Old and New Forms.

ALSO,

An Addreſs to Publicans, recommending to them to Adorn their Grounds with every requiſite Advantage, in Order to encourage, as much as poſſible, this uſeful and ſalutary Game.

By A. JONES, Eſq.

In Reaſon's Eye, the World's a Skittle Ground,
In which Mankind will tott'ring Pins be found:
The Bowl is Fortune, ſo be up who will,
It knocks them down by Hazard or by Skill.

LONDON.
Printed for the AUTHOR, and ſold by J. WILKIE, at N°. 71, in St. Paul's Church Yard.
MDCCLXXIII

[Price One Shilling.]

THE

PREFACE.

TO PUBLICANS, &c.

BEING brought up in my childhood in one of the most uncultivated parts of England, and since having had the opportunity of tasting the difference between that and the *finest or best polished* place, not only of this, but of most kingdoms in the known world; and that progressively, in the course of which I turned my mind, when tired from other observations and studies, to recreations of the soul, but found that I grew more tired with some than others; then I made observations on myself which I tired with soonest, and in general found, that after study, a game of exercise gave the greateſt and longeſt return to the tired faculties; and after labour, games of eaſe were beſt. At laſt I concluded that nature itſelf is but play, being only ſupported by action: a ſmith with his heavy hammer is tired by the continual labour, but when he is reſting himſelf with his arms acroſs, and leaning againſt the bench or wall, if he was commanded to keep that poſition for a conſiderable time, and was to be paid for it accordingly, he would tire as much with ſtanding ſtill as before with hard labour, and be glad to have his hammer again. From this obſervation it is natural to ſuppoſe, that games of relaxation for great towns full of people ſhould be rural and active, and the reverſe for people who labour hard. The games ſhould be proportioned to the labour which hath been gone through, and the time intended to be ſpent that way, or ill conſequences may enſue, ſuch as

ſpending

ſpending more time than can be ſpared, or of being tired before the time is expired.

It muſt be confeſſed, that for any great body of people it is hardly poſſible to find any recreation that ſhall be univerſal, as their employments are, and muſt be ſo various; but it is agreed by all, that thoſe are the moſt univerſal recreations, that give exerciſe to all the faculties at once.

The game or play at Nine-pins, or Skittles as it is commonly called, being the beſt adapted for a great and commercial city, I have given a full account of the ſame in all the forms I ſaw it played at, by all ſorts of people, and in all places I travelled through, whether under the name of Skittles, Nine-pins, Bowl-Ally, or any other appellation.

The reader will find here, the true methods of playing the game in old times, when it required more art than at prefent, and laid down in as plain language as the nature of the fubject will admit, which I wifh to have ftudied for the fake of recreation only, not with a defign to meet in order to guzzle and drink. To the credit of thofe publicans who have fkittle-grounds it may be fpoken, that one dozen of them prevent more drunkards than all the moral difcourfes put together. If labouring or confined men be tired with one fort of work, they muft have another, and for want of games, they drink without ceafing, while money and underftanding will hold out; but a game of recreation prevents that by the time required; and if the plans here laid down were renewed, then the games would be of longer duration, and more practifed, which would add much to the recreation of genteel tradefmen, as well as common labourers.

The

The Publicans, for whom this piece is chiefly intended, ought to do their endeavour to attempt the recovery of the game; this muſt be done though but by degrees, ſince it would be cramming a new ſyſtem down their players throats, and in conſequence they would loſe the idea of recreation, which muſt be the thing intended. While they endeavour to make their Grounds, &c. agreeable, for the good of their cuſtomers conſtitutions, &c. &c. then each will be of reciprocal advantage to the other, as well as honour to the game; and alſo will keep the nation clear of ſo many quack doctors to prey and eat up the vitals, as well as the money, that remain of the poor emaciated ſouls, loſt for want of air, exerciſe, &c.

I remain,
The Public
and Publicans'
Obedient humble Servant,

A. J.

THE ART OF PLAYING AT SKITTLES, &c.

OF GAMES IN GENERAL.

FROM the hiſtory of the world it may be obſerved, that as ſloth and idleneſs increaſe, ſo do the recreations of the ſoul; from active and manly exerciſes of the body, to thoſe of eaſe and lazineſs, which paſs under the more refined names of *genteel recreations*. If there was no other criterion of a body of people than that of their games or recreations to diſtinguiſh their genius by, that would be ſufficiently characteriſtic. The Grecians and Romans, when their youth were brought up with the manly exerciſes of leaping, jumping, running, wreſtling, and other feats of activity, were conquerors over all that oppoſed them; but when the more

genteel

genteel games came in faſhion, their youth became ſimilarly effeminate, and more of ſhadows than men. From this general change in the exerciſe of youth, comes that progreſſive arrival at effeminacy in every ſtate; therefore, it certainly muſt be better for the youth of every nation to be kept to manly exerciſes, and, as ſuch, ours ſhould follow Running, Leaping, Top-whipping, Marbles, &c. unto the age of ten or twelve; and after that age, the games of Priſon-baris, Foot-ball, Leaping, Skittles, Shuffle-board, with many more of exerciſe; all which are to be preferred to the genteel, refined, and lazy games of Cards, Dice, Back-gammon, Draughts, &c. &c. all of which were introduced by a luxurious and over-fed age of the people, when their ſouls were inſipid with eaſe and ſloth, and their bodies inactive from being over-fed with beef and plum-pudding, which naturally produce bog-bellies, ſwelled legs, gouty feet, and other ailments of a loaded corpſe, which are as much a diſgrace to mention, as they are for a patient to bear. This general change from games of activity to thoſe of eaſe, is evident

alſo

alſo in particular games, or the alterations made from the rural mode, to thoſe of art or ſcience, as they are termed; and if they happen not to have had men of ſcience to introduce a new faſhion, yet the people have fallen into the ſame from a mere inactive principle, or rather lazineſs, the mother of all ſhort methods and ways of eaſe to perform manual operations by.

In the northern counties of Northumberland, Weſtmoreland, Cumberland, Lancaſhire, Yorkſhire, &c. &c. &c. it is ſaid, that in old time, the greateſt diverſion of activity was with the Foot-ball, which received great encouragement from all the fathers of children, in order to inure their offspring to activity; but how far this game is relapſed from its original is evident. In old time, their balls were made of hay or ſtraw folded together perfectly round out of a thumb-rope *, which when looped, or knit through each quarter, makes the

* A Thumb-rope is one made by rolling the hay or ſtraw round the thumb, by moving the right hand, as the rope-makers do their twiſting mills.

the ball perfectly round, and by often kicking it at firſt in water, acquires a perfect hardneſs, with a little elaſticity, which is all that is required for this exerciſe. But in the moſt uncultivated parts, (as they are termed) theſe ſort of balls are but to be rarely ſeen now; for ſay the old people, *They hurt the toes of our bearns now, becauſe of their tender feet and thin ſhoes*; and in their ſtead is uſed a ſort made of horſe-hair hard beat into a four parted cover made of ſhoe-ſole leather. Theſe balls ſeem to have great art in them, as fitting better with the tender feet that is to drive them, but are not to be compared with the former and their players; who are always conquerors when in combat with the latter and their ball. However, either ſort are better than the laſt refinement, for with thoſe no trivial obſtacle will advantage the combatants by the rebound of the ball, ſuch as the wind, hedges, ſlender trees, and the like. I have ſeen round holes made through a buſh, or thickſet hedge, by thoſe balls, and alſo the opponents fly from them, dreading a blow from ſo hard a compoſition.

But

But according to the lateſt improvements, the balls are made of bladders, and in conſequence, are fit for the effeminate, fine, gentle, and *learned youth* of this age, to play in chambers with, or at the fire-ſide; not unlike a Liliputian in an egg-ſhell.

What has been particularized upon the manlike exerciſes of Foot-ball playing, might likewiſe be done upon ſeveral other ſorts of rural ſports, in their degeneracy from their deſign of exerciſe, to that of eaſe, ſuch as leaping upon a horſe inſtead of on the foot, and down inclined plains inſtead of level ground, becauſe the body will tumble down of itſelf; in Trap-ball, in hitting the ball with a flat board or round club, inſtead of a ſharp-edged one; and, laſtly, in the manly exerciſe of Skittle-playing, which I ſhall next particularize, and ſhew the great advantage to youth of all ſtations in life, eſpecially in its original rural form.

OF SKITTLE PLAYING.

IT has been allowed in all ages, by all the learned, that the bringing up of youth to a ſprightly and a lively imagination, or at leaſt to aſſiſt them for it, has been much forwarded by the games that they uſed in their recreations, and which have been moſtly thoſe that give a general action to all the parts of the body, from which the circulation will be more general through all the blood-veſſels.

For thoſe recreations in their youth, Top-whipping, or Setting, is allowed by the moſt ſenſible part of mankind to be the moſt proper exerciſe. Playing at Marbles is near of kin, but wants ſeveral poſitions of the body with the former, and what is worſe, that agility and ſprightlineſs of ſpirit required in it. In the ſtate of manhood we have no game ſo ſimilar, except that of Skittles, for in this there is much ſtooping, ſkipping, hitting marks, and (in the old games) catching with the

the hands, which naturally exerciſe all the faculties at once; and as there is a vacancy for replacing the game, or ſetting up the pins, the time will be ſufficient to refreſh the body in all its parts of exerciſe.

But what has been obſerved upon the decline of games in general from their modes of activity, to thoſe of a more genteel or eaſy method of performance, may be applied here; for the modern game of Skittles has no compariſon with its original, or, as it is called in ſome places, Nine-pins; and the old method of playing is in a manner intirely forgot, I ſuppoſe from its being too laborious, to this genteel and fine poliſhed age.

The old method has a great deal of art, activity, and ſcience in it, though the players or conſtructors might have no view in forming it but from mere chance *at firſt*, which is the caſe in all rural ſports whatever.

Their pins were nine as at preſent, but of different values or count, in proportion to their height and place in the frame; the pin which ſtands in the middle, has a head upon it in the form of a hat crown, with the lower part like the modern ones, but the whole pin, compoſed of the body and head, is higher than any of the others by the head. This pin was generally called King, or ſome other cant phraſe to the ſame ſenſe, ſuch as His Majeſty, Pin Royal. It counted for five.

The next in height and value, were the four corner pins, which were ſimilar to the King, with a head, and about three inches lower than him, and about as much higher than the other four, which ſtood in a line with them; theſe were called Dukes, Lords, Nobles, or by any cant names to the ſame meaning. Theſe four counted for three each when tipped by the King, or his conſequents, but if by the bowl or any other from it, either of their own height or lower, they only counted for two each.

The remaining four were called Common, or Commons, and counted for two each when tipped by the King, but by any other

only

only one each. All tips or knock-downs in consequence of other pins rolling from those that knock'd them down, the same as in the common game now played.

The frame was not in the form now used, but the present seems to be the remains of it; for in the old game there was a square frame round the square of the pins, which is now called the frame. This will be best represented by a diagram which was not unlike the figure in page 24, in which that part represented by the square figure A B C D, was the frame, and the other was only called the square of the pins, which now is called the frame.

In this figure, the King, Lords, and Commons, are evident from their several distinct marks of black, shaded, and white, which must be used for the sake of determining the several games to come.

The distance of the pins and in-frame were fixed in a just proportion from the out-frame and each other to agree with the height of the pins, though done by mere chance or experience, I found, upon meaſuring of ſeveral frames, that they kept an exact mathematical proportion, ſo as to form the properties of the parabola, or in plain words, that the ſpaces from pin to pin and the out-frame were thoſe which the bowl would deſcribe, with a force equal to its weight, in falling from the height of the pins.

The frames are fixed upon perfect plains, and the bowl has no bias in it; all the different tips are acquired by the out-frame, which is compoſed of four different pieces of hard wood, though ſome have them of hard ſmooth ſtones when they can be eaſily come at.

The breadths of the ſides of theſe frames were in general about ſix inches, and inclined on their out-ſurface about half a right angle, or forty-five degrees at the moſt, but all the ſides were not alike, that from their different inclinations, the bowl might be made to hit

a higher

a higher or lower pin in proportion; this is for the advantage of the players, that they may take any advantageous pin that offers from the inclination of the fides.

The great art of this game is in hitting the out-frame fo that the bowl may be made to hit any intended pin, which is come at by the pofition of the body or hand to the frame, and great experience. The bowl running againft the middle of the frame in a right line, and at right angles to the fame, will rife in proportion to the force and refiftance of the out-frame, and by inclining the line of direction, or making a lefs angle with the frame, the bowl will have a contrary direction among the pins, fo that it may be made to hit the corner pins or thofe in a right line with it, and either in a direct or oblique direction, fo as to hit any favourite pin at pleafure.

The bowl and tip in this game are near alike, for the fame number may be got in both; the King-pin is made heavier than any of the other by near one half, and the bowl as heavy as the King very near, or as about the numbers 8 to 9. These are the first general principles of this old game.

The particulars must be varied according to the general laws of the probability of winning to those of losing, which must be a mean of the sum of the greatest and least go; and also their particular exceptions of hits or misses, so as to form what may be called a lawful go. With those that I have practised with, the law of a fair go is, to hit the frame at the going in, and not to touch it within, or hit, as it is called; and also to take up or put out of the way useless or dead pins. The greatest go that can be had (as will be found farther on) is 40, or 20 at the bowl and the same at the tip; the least go must be 1, so the mean is 20, therefore the guift law must be 6, for the first within the power of the frame, and the game must be 61.

As to particular exceptions or variations, they may have been according to the choice of the ſeveral players; but from what I have obſerved, where any remains are to be found of this old and noble game, that its laws have been always the ſame, or nearly ſo.

I once ſaw a curious piece of antiquity, ſhewing the original law of this game, which was a frame made of oak, with the general rules to be obſerved cut upon it, and which was juſt legible. Upon the taking down of an old hall near Ribcheſter, in Lancaſhire, in part of it there was a window of twelve feet ſquare, the frame of which had been a ſkittle-frame, from the evident marks found upon it, giving the laws of the game: each ſide of the frame was nine inches broad, with inclinations of 50, 60, 70, and 80 degrees reſpectively: upon the upper edges of the frame were 61 holes, in two rows, one of which had a blank of 6 after 40; with theſe lines round the frame:

"Bowl ſtrong, hit the frame without, and miſs the ſame within,
"The King, two Lords, with their attendants, the game will bring."

A. D. 1486.

From this inſcription, it is certain of what great antiquity the game muſt be; and how much of it remains now is evident, ſince we have little more than the ſhadow left.

Alſo from the above deſcription it muſt be plain, that the bowl was to hit the King and two Lords, with whom, and their attending rowls, the game would be won. But this muſt mean the principal bowls and tips, or goes. To confirm which, I obſerved in the aforeſaid frame, that it was guttered in the middle of each ſide, and about two feet from each corner, by the hitting of the bowl againſt the frame; but more at the corners than in the ſeveral middles; which made me conclude from theſe marks, and what I have experienced myſelf, that the beſt players always attempted their goes in diagonals of the frame, or from corner to corner, but

rather

rather with an oblique motion, that the force of reſiſtance given by the King, returned the bowl upon the right-hand Lord, in conſequence of which, the whole frame was cleared. This would not be poſſible, unleſs the King was heavy enough to be equal to the remaining force of the bowl.

Now we arrive at the real practice of the game, it may be obſerved from the nature of it, that the bowls and tips will have different names; ſuch as, the Royal Tip, nine, ten, eleven, twelve, &c. &c. Noble Tip, two, three, four, &c. and all the reſt common.

For the eaſe of the reader, the following figure is referred to when wanted.

I will

I will now begin with the Grand go.

The firſt, or Grand go.

Fig. 1.

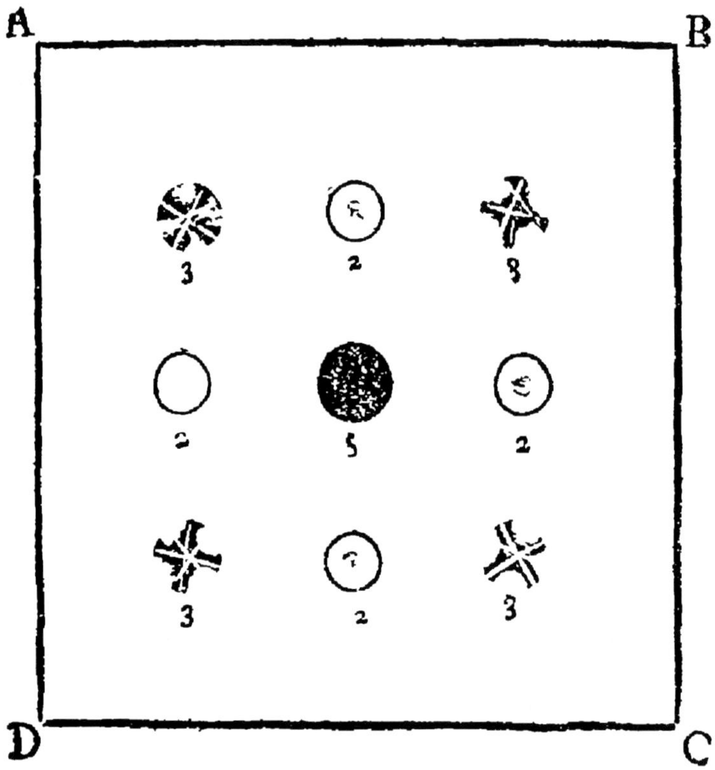

From this figure, and what has been delivered before upon the general principles of the game, may be formed the intent of the firſt go. It muſt be noted, that the player is not bound to any particular diſtance with the bowl, nor to any corner or ſide of the frame,

frame, but is at liberty to chuſe the ſide and diſtance he thinks he can raiſe the curve to bring the moſt at his go. Having choſe his diſtance, ſide, (we will ſuppoſe D C) and angle required, which ſhould firſt be well experienced, then he will begin to hit the Noble at D, from whence the bowl will paſs to the King, and from thence will be reflected back to the Noble at C, when being ſpent, will move towards B, and moſt likely will bring down Common B C, or Noble at B.

But if it hits Noble B, moſt likely the game will be loſt, unleſs the player immediately leaps into the frame to catch the bowl, which is always attempted, to prevent it hitting, rubbing, or touching, as it is moſt commonly called. This I have ſeen done by active young men, when the bowl has had too great a force, and would have drove the pegs out of the frame that the count was kept by. It is from the ſeveral heights, weights, as well as baſes of the pins, that cauſes the natural reflection of the bowl. Theſe four are properly the bowl pins, and by the law of count come to 2, 5, 2, and 1, the ſum of which is 10.

The pins in conſequence are evident, for the firſt Lord will naturally roll in a curve line from D corner to A D 2; the King, by his great power, will overthrow the Common A B, and Lord B, where he will fall, with his head on the inclined plain, which will give him a force to roll up towards A B till he traverſes to the Lord at A, if that pin is not beat down by the Common A B.

This will be quite natural to his majeſty, for in the return he will take a larger arc, and in conſequence will come with a greater force upon both. I have ſeen the Noble at A, recoil ſo ſtrong from his majeſty, as to bring down the Common at A D, when miſſed by the bowl pin at D. The laſt pin in conſequence is from the Lord at C, it will be natural to him to roll round upon D C Common.

By

By the laws of count, these pins are 2, 3, 3, from the King, and from the inferiors 1 and 1, which is 2, therefore the whole sum is 10; and of the bowl and tip it must be 20. The principal aim in this bowl or tip is to hit the King, because him and his attendants count so many; therefore little care is taken of the first Noble, as he and his followers come all from the bowl; but to hit the King without moving him round upon his base, so that he may have no attendants, is one of the worst bowls or tips that can be made. He ought to spin round upon his base before he falls at the Common A B, and by that means will bring that pin down, and in his rolls perform the rest as has been explained.

The above, when performed, is the Royal go by reflection; it bears this name not only if 20 is brought, but also if any of the pins are missed, as is often the case, then it is called Royal go, 19, 18, 17, &c. or the goes and tips are mentioned so, as Royal go 6, 8, &c. and Royal tip 7, 8, 6, &c.

By this diſtinction being regiſtered, it prevents diſputes.

But by reaſon of the great difficulty of performing the foregoing bowl or tip, it more frequently turns into the next in honour and value; which ſhall be next explained.

In this go, the bowl hits the Nobles at D and B, and in paſſing ſpins the King, which three pins count 2, 5, and 2, or 9. The pins in conſequence are A B Common, and A Noble, from the King, for he will roll between them, and bring down A B Common, and fall with his head upon the inclined plain, which will roll to A Noble; from the bowl, D Noble upon A D Common, and by his roll, D C Common, from B Noble B C Common, excluſive of vibrating rolls. The count of this go is, for the King 5, and 4 for the bowl, makes 9; the pins in conſequence are 2 from the Noble D, 2 and 3 from the King, and 1 from the Noble B; upon B C Common, or the whole

ſum,

ſum, is 17 for the go or tip, and the ſum of both, or the whole go, is 34.

It is called a go, or tip royal direct, with the numbers that it brings.

There is great dexterity and nimbleneſs in this go; for the player will be very liable to let the bowl hit the frame from its line of direction, and at the ſame time muſt remove the dead pin A B Common out of the way of the King in his way to the Noble at A.

The next go is the Noble by reflection, which ſhall be next explained.

The art of this go or tip, is to hit the Noble at D, in a line to the King, who will reflect the bowl to the Noble at A, from whence it will roll round to the noble at B, in a curve line. The Noble B may be looked upon as a conſequence, becauſe the bowl will roll from A to B, which it ſeldom does in bowl pins. The conſequence pins are A D, A B, and B C, Common, from their ſeveral Lords D, A, and B, and often the Lord C, with his Common from the King. The count for the whole is from the King, 5, 3, 2; and from the bowl, 1, 1, 2, 1, 2, and 1; or their ſum is 8, and the whole go or tip muſt be 18.

If the King falls only, and has no attendants, the bowl or tip is called, Noble; but if otherwiſe, it is Noble Royal.

The next go is of equally great art with any of the former, though of not the ſame proportionate number; it is called Noble Direct, from the direct Nobles being the bowl pins. The bowl in this go, muſt be raiſed to hit one of the Nobles, as at D or C, when it will fly over A D, or B C Common; and will take the oppoſite Lord (as ſuppoſe at B) and may perhaps take the Common B C; all the conſequence pins will be A B, and D C Common; but if the bowl ſhould happen to roll from C Lord to B the ſame, then it will moſt likely return to the frame, and what it brings is allowed, as an induce-

ment

ment of hitting on purpose for a miss-go or tip. This is the only go that the bowl is allowed to return into the frame, for it is only played upon the close of the game, and therefore the allowance is as above. The count, without the return of the bowl, is 6 for the two Lords, and 2 in consequence are 8.

The last principal go is called Common Direct; the chief art in this, is to hit the King with great force, that he may roll much about, and have many attendants, or pins in consequence, to raise the game. It is plain, that in this go there are only two bowl pins, D C Common, and the King, for the other Common is mostly missed, from the difficulty in forming the arc. The King by his motion will go between A B Common and B Lord, and will bring down B C, and A B Common in his first roll; also A Lord and A D Common, in his second.

The

The count is, from the bowl 6, and in consequence of the King alone, 3, 2, 2, 3, 2, or 12; and the whole go or tip is 18.

This go seems as advantageous as any, since there may be great numbers got from it; but without great force be given the King, he is of no use but himself; then there will be no more in count than the two bowl pins; and if he be hit over hard, the bowl cannot be catched if it should happen to incline to the frame; therefore this go is never attempted but upon a little number wanted.

All other goes are called Common, as having in them generally more Common pins than any other sort. Though some of them might very properly be called Common by reflection. As it was immaterial what side was chose to illustrate the games, I all along have supposed the side D C the play side, as shewing the different paths best, when compared with one another. But now it must be evident, that any side will

do,

do, or may be taken, ſince there are the ſame numbers at each of them, and the ſame bowls and tips, &c.

Now I will illuſtrate ſome of the common goes: but firſt of the Common by Reflection (as it may be called) though not by that name.

It is plain that from any ſide the bowl may play from 2, bowl King, and be reflected to 2 or 3 acute or oblique; in the firſt the King will roll oppoſite 3, and right-hand, and oppoſite 2; the whole count of which will be 7 for bowl, 3, 2, and 2, or 9 for the King, the whole of which will be 16, and the whole go 32; though this may often miſs from the King, who may not roll ſo many. The bowl for 3 acute will be 8, the whole for the go muſt be 16.

The bowl for 3 oblique will be 2, 5 and 3, which are 8, as in the acute caſe; and the roll from the King will be 5, on the right,

right, which is 13, and the whole go will be 26.

Theſe are all the principal goes in common; any others may be had at pleaſure; ſuch as a 2 from the middle of the frame, by two common or one three in either corner, and by the ſame three pins, 5 by the King, 6, 7, 8, 9, &c. &c. have been ſhewn in the other tips aforegoing.

The foregoing is the wh le of this game, in all its general and particular goes, for the moſt general ſport; but there is another form, that affords as much diverſion as the one explained.

Which is, to move the Nobles into the place of the Commons, and *vice verſa*. This game is much eaſier, as the King will always be among the Nobles, and the *in conſequence* pins will be more numerous and beſt at the beginning of a game, as following from him alone, but the tips have the ſame names,

and

and are of the ſame number, as well Royal, Noble, as Common.

Though the frame for the game be placed upon level ground, yet the ſpace between the two frames was banked round with earth, or ſome of the beſt hard boards laid like an inclined plain all round, which makes the bowl and pins to have a natural roll, the former of which was prevented from hitting, and the latter made to have a natural tendency to roll, ſo that the pins in conſequence were often more than was expected, and alſo made many chance bowls and tips be equal to the beſt conceited and executed ſort, which gave an indifferent player a greater chance for a ſingle game or two.

From this plain and full explanation of the original of this old game, and what it is now, may be noticed, as I ſaid, the degeneracy of this age, and what a pitiful pattern we have of it, a form that has neither genius nor art in it, at leaſt as it is generally practiſed, though it plainly ſhews its defcending from the old form aforegoing. For the ground is generally banked round, to caufe a rolling of the bowl and pins; but the art, for the feveral degrees of bowls and tips, feems entirely loft; and, in general, if two moderate players begin, the chance of the game refts upon which gets the go, and that is obtained by the tofs of a halfpenny, fo the game in confequence is reduced to the fame.

It is not poffible for any body of people to leave an old cuftom off all at once; but when a general plan of improvement is laid down, it may be followed by degrees when clearly underftood; and as fuch, our modern game of fkittles may be improved by the foregoing old plan.

Firft, for the players to be allowed a triangular piece of wood, fo that it might be fhifted to any part of the frame, by bowling and tipping againft it, the bowl would rife, and would form feveral of the bowls and tips as laid down before in the old game, but in particular the direct ones, if the pins were made one higher than another, the reflected tips would alſo be come at without more trouble; and if they were alſo made of different weights, we ſhould be nearer the old principle, truth, and plan.

Thus to bowl with the pins ſo altered, and with the triangular block to imitate the Royal by reflection;—The three diagonal pins would be certain if no reflection happened, which would have two chances;—if in the middle pin, then the bowl reflected would be certain of two to the right, if not more, and the middle pin could not miſs the oppoſite corner, beſides its' rolls, which by all the laws of this game, there would be a certainty of two, therefore the whole bowl would make ſeven. It muſt be now admitted, that the tip would, by common reaſon, be eight, if not the whole nine, therefore the general go would be fifteen, which is little leſs than one and a half of what is commonly got.

Any ſingle tip to make up the game would be come at in a moſt certain manner, as this would be obtained by barely ſhifting the block, ſo that the bowl would not knock down more than what is wanted; therefore it behoves the players of this game to get maſter of this great and laſt improvement, both for the exerciſe of their ſeveral faculties, and alſo to cauſe their games to be of greater recreation.

If we now leave all addition to the modern form of playing, but make a philoſophical obſervation upon the methods uſed in the old game, we ſhall naturally come into the beſt goes and tips in the former. In the old game, the pins were of a height to form a regular arch for riſing and falling bodies, that if the bowl roſe regular to hit the middle pin, thence, in a ſimilar arch, it would naturally do the ſame in its deſcent; the weight of the pins cauſed a natural reflection of the bowl, which often produced uncommon and unexpected goes and tips, but eſpecially the former. The diſtance of the

the pins was ſuch, that each might be a conſequence from its ſuperior; ſo that if the King alone was hit, the player might have a good chance to bring the whole frame. The King ſhould, in falling, be of the length that his ſhoulder in ſtooping might be above the centre of gravity of his hitting pin, and that pin the ſame to the next, and ſo on to the end; but this is determined by their diſtance, and that beſt found by the maker, who forms the heights, &c. The frame of the old one, cauſeth the bowl to riſe, by which the arch for the top of the pins was formed.

As the modern game has none of the above advantages, in conſequence we are not to expect the tips, &c. from them, but what can be raiſed by art in imitation of them.

The pins being all of one weight, there can be no go by reflection, therefore all muſt be direct; as there is no frame, the bowl cannot be raiſed but by the management of the player, &c.

Therefore as our game now ſtands, with its mode of playing, for the go, the beſt is for the bowl to riſe or hop at going in, and, if poſſible, to hit the edge of the frame, if the corner pin is miſſed; but it ſhould be attempted a little above the middle, ſo that the bowl may have a ſecond hop upon the middle pin, and if ſo, it is fifty to one but there will be a third, and ſometimes (if the bowl be ſpent) by reflection, which will cauſe a general fall of the pins, at leaſt there cannot be leſs than a fall of ſix, though I have ſeen more, and even the whole nine; to obtain which, the bowl ſhould be played over knotty ground, if there is any in it. It is uſual to go ſtrait through, and in general to bring only at a mean two or three, and theſe often with a hit or rub.

The tips are eaſy, and are only a conſequence of the old go or tips direct; but as the player can chuſe the ground, he gives his hand a reflected twiſt, and by that means takes all the pins down he intends. All the art is the deſigned pins, and hitting with force. But if the bowl could be made to have a natural undulated motion, and not be ſo ſtrong, alſo that the pins might be hit nearer the top, or at leaſt above the centre of gravity of their falling; then the tips would be more certain of number when wanted.

Of the CHINESE Game.

IT is imagined by many who pretend to the principles of virtue and ſobriety, that the game of ſkittles is the produce of beer-houſes, and, in conſequence, think it an inducement to idleneſs, and inſtead thereof adviſe inactive games, ſuch as cards, dice, draughts, &c.

But we find that ſome of the moſt ſenſible nations in the world have the ſame game in uſe, as the Chineſe and Perſians; though it muſt be allowed, that theſe have in a great meaſure (through eaſe and falſe délicacy) loſt the original intention, which was undoubtedly for the exerciſe of youth.

The Chineſe plan is to have twenty-five pins, which makes the next odd ſquare above nine. As far as I can gather from hiſtory, they had the ſame uſe of the frame as before laid down, and differed only in the number of pins and the plain upon which they ſtood, which formed a perfect fruſtrum of a concave ſphere of a particular radius or curvature, in proportion to the Kings (for they had five of them, though of different count) and their height, as well as the ſize of the heads. To form the conſtruction of all the parts with preciſion, would require no leſs than a mathematical calculation. But a general plan, with an explanation, may ſuffice here *.

* The reader is to take notice, that the annexed plan, as well as that which follows, have not their proportionate diſtances, for want of room; but he may have a proper idea how to form each from the plan of the common one, or Fig. 1.

The Plan. Fig. 2.

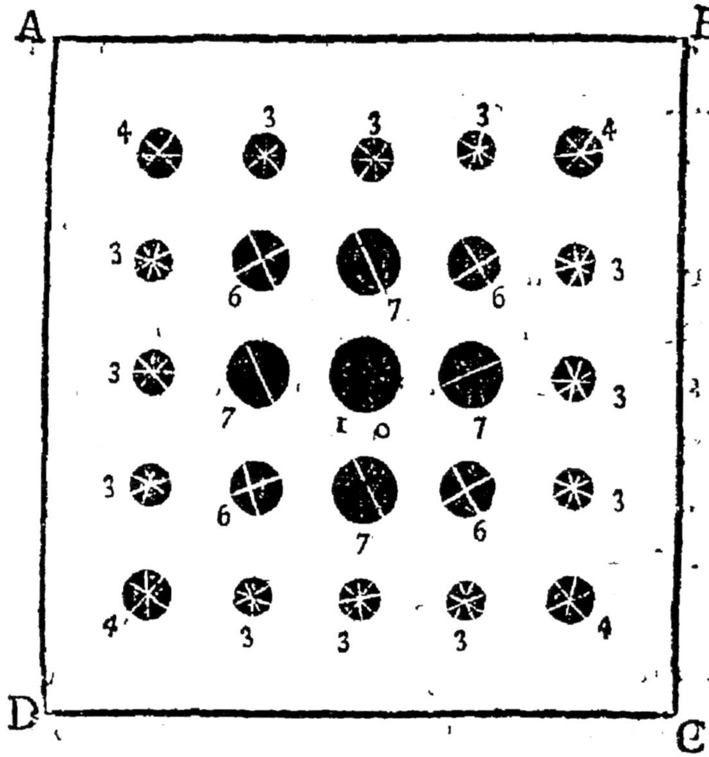

From this diagram it is plain, that our form of the game is only a contraction of it; which will appear when the nature of this is a little explained. The pin marked 10, for which it counts, is the King or Emperor; the four crossed ones, marked 7 each, are so many petty Kings or Deputies; the four marked 6, are Nobles,

Nobles, as before in our game; and the four marked 4 at each corner, are their Deputies or attendants; all thoſe marked 3, are Common. Each pin counts for its marked number, when got by the Emperor or his four inferiors; but by the Nobles, &c. or the bowl, they loſe one from each. The height and weight of the pins are as the numbers marked upon each; ſo that their tops may form an arch proportionate to their diſtances, and that their weights may be able to anſwer their numbers; ſuch as that two of 7 may be ſuperior to 10, and ſo on through the whole. The crowns of the ſuperiors are proportionate to the curve of the frame, in order for each pin to have a natural tendency to vibrate from one ſide of the frame to the other, and yet to ſhift their centres. The weight of the bowl is eight parts of the middle pin 10.

The outs of this game are not ſo many as ours; for all that is required is for the bowl to hit the outſide of the frame, and when out of the pins, not to return, whe-

ther

ther it hits the frame or not; in going out it is no matter, ſince the form is conſtructed for this purpoſe chiefly; nor indeed would it be poſſible to catch a bowl, ſince the frame muſt be very large when conſtructed upon a little ſcale.

Laſtly, four on a ſide muſt play at this game, that there may always be three to take up dead pins.

The game is 457, which is to be got at one go, including both go and tip. As each player has an equal fair chance, by their alternate goes, there is no guiſt bowl in it.

Though it may ſeem as if the game would be certain to one party, yet the art conſiſts in not coming too near, but that it will come in by ſome certain tip which offers; and though each party may be 1, 2, 3, &c. before, the ſame may loſe, as thinking to bring them to a tip within reach, yet not one in a thouſand may be able to get it;

and

and it often may happen that neither ſide arrive at the game, but both begin a-new: theſe are called blank games, which if they happen to 13, without ever having one proper, the preference is always given to the majority in that number that came the neareſt to one proper.

To ſhew the ſimilarity between our game and this, I gave the pins ſimilar names; but the Chineſe call them by the ſeveral names of Tong-hhu, Tſi-ſhu, Pela-ſhu, Tye-limu, and Nang-mu, becauſe of the ſimilarity of the pins when ſtanding to a wood; which names may, with great propriety, be modified to ſuit us into this order and abbreviations, viz. Tong-u, Ty-u, Tiſ-u, Pel-u, Hang-u; which names have a near affinity to, I command you, I tye you, I teaſe you, I compel you, and I hang you. The very language from Emperors to Kings, from Kings to Lords, from Lords to attendants, and their attendants to the commons, who have the hanging or cutting off of all the formers heads; which names, when abbreviated

viated again, will naturally be only the firſt words of each name, or perhaps ſhorter.

These names being known, then any particular bowl or tip will have a name alſo, by which means each may be regiſtered, to prevent diſputes in the game. This being premiſed, I ſhall begin with the tips.

The firſt go or tip is Tong-u Royal, and is no more than hitting him with the force and art to roll round his baſe, and fall upon his four inferiors, 7 each, in his roll, who will each have a ſimilar motion, and fall upon their inferiors; in like manner the next will do the ſame to theirs, down to the loweſt, and all will come down, which will be in conſequence of Tong-u; therefore the count will be 114.

The ſecond is Tong-u by reflection, which muſt be made from the ſide D C, by the bowl pins 4, 6, 10, direct, and the reflected ones 6, in a line with C, and between two 3's towards B, when the bowl will roll and carry off 4, at B corner. The confequence pins, by following the bowl, are 4 at D corner, upon the firft 3 to the left, and both of them upon the next. The next bowl-pin, 6, with the affiftance of thofe already down from 4, will overthrow the 7 to the left; and he by his power will overthrow the pin 6 towards A, who by the affiftance of his fuperior, will bring down all that corner. Then Tong-u, 10, will overthrow oppofite 7, and by his refiftance will be reflected to 6, and fo on to B C 7. The confequence pins from C 6 are 4, C, and two 3's on D C, whofe power bring down D C 7, who clears that fide and corner, if any be left. The confequence from middle 3, B C, is C 3, and laftly from 4 B, two 3's on A B, and perhaps the whole three.

The count from the bowl-pins are 3, 5, 10, 5, 2, 2, 3; that from the in confequence to Tong-u, 7, 6, 7, for himfelf, and from C 6; 3, 2, 22, 6, 2; from middle 3, B C 2, and from B, 4, 2, 2.

In

In like manner the pins in A D ſide, &c. are counted. The ſum of the whole is 91. This is upon the ſuppoſition of the pins following their law from a good player. But it is very frequent for oppoſite 7 to overthrow A, 6; and, in conſequence, they two clear all that corner, which quite changes the game, for inſtead of 2, 3, 2, 5, they count 3, 4, 3, and 6; beſides, if the gatherers are expert, they alſo cauſe a great difference, from thoſe that are not; for it often happens that Tong-u will perform near the ſame of the firſt Tip, &c.—From the laſt go may be learned a different way of gaining the firſt go or royal Tong-u, which it is called by way of pre-eminence, as has been ſaid. The whole art in this go, is to miſs all the pins but 10, and he muſt be hit with a direction between two of his inferiors, with a roll upon his baſe, as if he was going to fall; by which motion he will begin with oppoſite 7 (from D C) and proceed round to A 6, upon which he will fall, (if not down from one 7) and thence will roll round and take the remaining 6's. But upon Tong-u moving his inferiors, they each of them will bring down their inferiors on the four 6's, and theſe laſt will each carry the corner D's 4's, which will bring all the Commons by their rolling to and again. This counts all royal Tong-u, or 114. If the pins which appear certain to be of no uſe but as dead ones be taken up, upon a fair fall, and Tong-u be fairly hit, this go will be eaſily maſtered.

The next go is one that naturally comes from miſſing the firſt, which is to hit ſome of the pins that were to have been miſſed, and is generally to hit D 6, by reflection 7, Tong u 10, 7 B C, 6, and 3 B. The conſequence pins are from 7, 7, C 6, two 3's one 4, from D, 6, two 3's, one 7; from Tong-u, 7, A B, two 3's, one 4, and one 6; from 6 B one 3, and one 4; all of which, when counted, will come to (from the bowl) 5, 6, 10, 6, 5, 2, or 34. The conſequences to the right are 19, and to the left 45, all of which are 98. This bowl and tip is called Double Direct Tong-u.

The

The next go is called Direct Tong-u, from its being made from corner to corner, which is a very eafy go, though attended with great numbers, as will appear. The bowl is played from any 4, to its oppofite; and when the bowl-pins are hit from the fides, they will all move anglewife towards A. But here they muft be boldly ftruck, and the confequences will be, all thofe on the left, from Tong-u, oppofite 7, B C 7, with its confequences, which will bring moft of the right-hand fide, as may be underftood from the other goes.

This bowl or tip is generally from 85 to 90 or 93.

The next and only go as a principal is Tong-u Ty-u direct, which is evident muft be made from the fides of the fquare, with 3, 7, Tong-u, 10, 7, 3. The difficulty of this go is in defcribing the arch required; for it muft be very much curved, in order to hit the two 3's, but if they be miffed, it matters little, fince they will come down by their ſuperiors. The general numbers of this go are from 50 to 70, or 75.

All the others, or inferiors, are evident; that is, ſuch as 2, 3, 4, &c. to 20, which are reckoned as a ſingle and certain number to get, and therefore the game is granted, the ſame as we do when one is wanted.

Of the PERSIAN Game.

THE Perſian game, tho' not of the ſame ingenuity and contrivance as the former, yet has its beauties; there are only 17 pins here, but to have them five in a row, they are placed in concentric circles, with one pin in the centre, which is called the King or Emperor, as before.

The circles are three in number; in the neareſt ſtand the petty Kings, and ſo on as in the Chineſe ſcheme before explained.

In this game there is no out-frame, but the baſe of the in-one is exactly the ſame, with

with the pins of the ſame proportion, height, weight, and bowl, in proportion to the principal. The numbers of theſe pins are 9, 7, 5, 3; choſe, I ſuppoſe, from their being odd, which was one of the Eaſtern whimſies, with many others that they entertained upon theſe numbers.

Fig. 3.

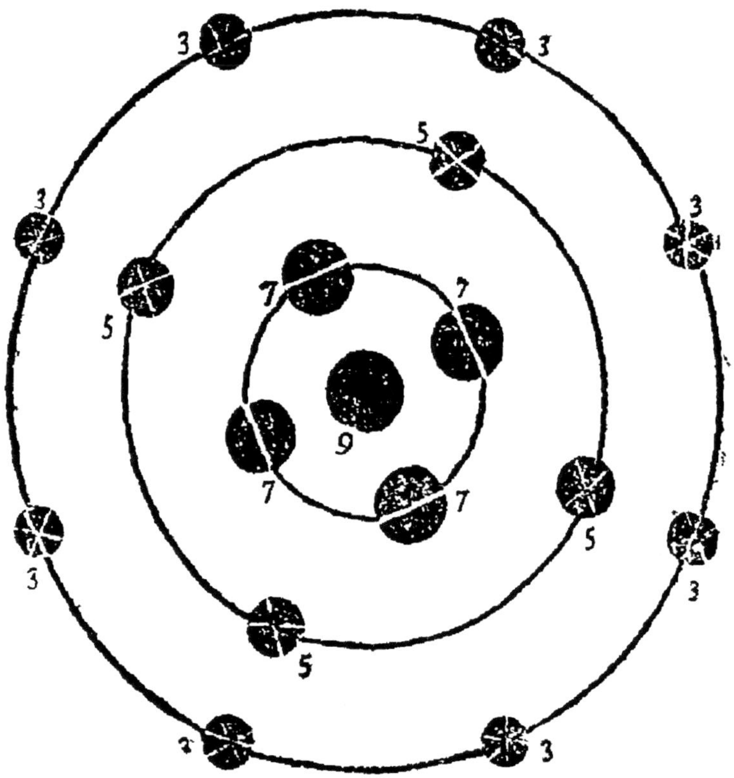

In this game they only bowl, and the bowl has a bias in it, which is played to carry as many of the 3's as poſſible in the out circle, before it inclines to the inner one of 5's; and alſo to enter in at the ſame part oppoſite, as if the bowl entered at 3 to the righ , then it ſhould enter again at 5 in the ſame radius, that by this ſimilar motion it may enter again between two 7's on the ſame ſide, and come at the King free from hitting the pins 7, by which means more will fall from the King than bowl; and alſo he will fall towards the ſide of the ſtanding pins, and in conſequence will get more than all. The difference between the bowl-falls and thoſe of the King is 2 upon each pin, as is plain from their common difference, the former therefore is of little value to the latter.

The diſtance to be ſtood at is arbitrary, or as the parties agree, and alſo the game is formed from the number that it is poſſible to be got at a determined number of goes.

Some

Some play at this game with banked ground, like our common ſkittle grounds, and others with quite flat, the ſame as a room floor, or upon a floor itſelf. I need not be ſo particular in this game, as it is well underſtood by many, eſpecially in the northern counties, where it goes under the name of Rouly Pouly, and is played with great art, and variety of different games, which may be called ſo many different goes in the ſame game.

But if the pins be made as conſequences of each other, as I have alſo ſeen them done, then the King ought to be hit firſt by a hop of the bowl, or by moving among the pins in a curve line between any two 3's, the next 7 and 5 farther off, and turn in between the two next 7's, by which the King will overthrow his four inferior 7's, they their four 5's, and the fives their inferior threes, which will be natural, if the pins be made of a right height to each other; for each five at his fall will bring down its oppoſite 3, and by its roll the other. A whole go in this

this case is 81, which is certain to be obtained, if the bowl hops either over the inferior pins or through them, so as to miss them all, and hit the King near the top or head.

ERRATUM.

Page 48, last line but one, for 22, read 2.

FINIS.